In *Postcards* [...] and forth like two professional tennis players locked in a championship match of poetics. Only here the ball is a river, a creek, a sound, a machine, a myth, and the racquets that power the game are called Environment, Natural Disaster, God, Glaciers and Grass. All this beauty—in one game.
> —Xavier Cavazos, **Barbarians at the Gate**,
> *Poetry Society of America*

These poems between friends begin with a casualness I very much like, but the skill in language and the strong image resonance throughout are what pulled me back and back for more. . . . Hearing echoes I wasn't sure of, remembering a translucence of water from somewhere earlier, were unexpected enticements I found in these poems. The *skin of memory* from one of them is apt here: balm, prickling, along with a shiver of feather stroke now and then... I will carry these in the skin of memory long after reading the poems.
> —Dixie Partridge, **Deer in the Haystacks**,
> *Poetry of the West*

This series of volleying poems from two brothers in poetry produces both connections and contrasts. Their poems address nature, myth, place, relationships and belief, but always at the center of the collection is the gentle profundity of human life. The often-subtle hand-off between poems engages the reader as a novel rather than a compilation, so much so that the end arrives with sudden regret.
> —Karen Bonaudi, **Editing a Vapor Trail**,
> *Pudding House Press*

To the Stanciks —
Enjoy!

POSTCARDS FROM JIM

A Correspondence of poems

Jim Thielman

Jim Thielman
and
Jim Hanlen

Copyright © 2015 Jim Thielman & Jim Hanlen

All rights reserved. No part of this book may be used or reproduced by any means, graphic, electronic, or mechanical, including photocopying, recording, taping or by any information storage retrieval system without the written permission of the publisher except in the case of brief quotations embodied in critical articles and reviews.

ISBN-13: 978-1514879313
ISBN-10: 151487931X

Acknowledgements

Jim Hanlen

Iraqi Bird Census *Cirque* Vol 2 No 1 2010
Looking Under Yeats Bed *Cirque* Vol 3 No 1 2011
Fukushima Japan 2011 in *Flyways* 2012
River Dance *Puget Sound Papers* 2012
Current Map For Hugo *Cirque* Vol 5 No 1 2013
Unnamed Creek Behind Cavazos House *Cirque* Vol 6
        No 1 2014
Williams' Chickens *Cirque* Vol 6 No 1 2014
Outside EZ Loader 1966 Cirque Vol 6 No 2 2015

Jim Thielman

Balm for Blind Hearts in *America* October 1986
When You Picture *Cirque* Vol 4 No 2 2012
Rising *Cirque* Vol 6 No 1 2014

Brenda Jaeger	Cover Art: *Weather Moving In*
Jim Thielman	Book and Cover Design
Shelly Senator, Dan Clark	Editorial Review

Dedication

To our wives
who encouraged and endured
through the long creative process.

Pat Thielman
and
Brenda Jaeger

Introduction

      Jim Thielman asked Jim Hanlen about writing a book of poems together, much like Marvin Bell and William Stafford's book *Segues*, poetry as a form of correspondence. Originally, they decided to call the book *Sequels.* The thought was that the poems would follow each other and borrow a word or two from the previous poem. It was Thielman's artist friend, Thelma Tripplet who suggested the title *Postcards*, when she heard that the poems were sent back and forth, although of course today, the sending was electronic. Dan Clark of Thielman's writing group also contributed, providing articles on putting a book of poetry together.

      The greatest benefit of the collaboration would turn out to be prompting each other to write more. In the end, they produced more than 120 poems, but as they neared the end of the project, they opted for a selection of poems they liked best, 29 poems from each author, 58 poems total. Together they also decided to further free themselves up and substitute poems here and there that seemed a better fit. The emphasis was on putting out the best book they could.

Once the poems were collected, they began a review to see where they should go. Many of the poems written as sequels fit together consecutively, as originally planned. But with a printout of the poems, Thielman played with the arrangement several times, until he saw a connection in every two poems as they are presented here. Two by two, the poems march through the book like animals climbing onto Noah's Ark, and not necessarily better behaved, because they wanted poems alive with spirit and they believe they have them.

During the review, their editors, Dan Clark and Shelly Senator reminded them to think of the reader first not the writer. So, they altered the order of the poems to pick a collection that would pull readers into the collection with the enticements of surprising subjects and unique points of view.

Thielman and Hanlen are longtime friends, having met in elementary school in Spokane and continued at the same schools through Gonzaga University. In their working life, they both lived for a time in Richland, Washington. Thielman is still there, while Hanlen now lives in Anchorage, Alaska.

You can see in the poems a connection to the natural beauty of the Northwest, including rivers and creeks. But you also see wide ranging imaginations dealing with the stuff of lives that began in the mid-1940s and went through the amazing changes that have occurred since then.

We hope you enjoy reading the book they discovered as they journeyed together toward its completion.

Contents

When You Picture..1
Outside Seaside High School...2

Uncle Fritz..3
Five Hand Shadows of Birds Thrown Upon a Wall...................4

Dances With Grandma...5
River Dance..6

Prometheus Resigned..7
Outside the Gates..8

Animals are Buddhists Too...9
Creek Carried the Moon...10

Balm for Blind Hearts...11
Blind Priest...12

Bike Ride on Padero Lane..14
Professor Gilmore's Breakfast Lecture..................................15

Do-It-Yourself Traction...16
Romanian Circus...18

This Letter..20
Another Way to Read a Poem...21

River Talk...22
River Breath...23

Turtle Man..24
Looking Under Yeats' Bed..25

EZ Loader 1969...26
Outside EZ Loader 1966...27

Peaceful Valley 1967...28
Water Ave, Peaceful Valley...30

Bliss..31
Fukushima, Japan 2011...32

Inside Game..33
Longevity...34

The Story of My Life..35
Want of Miracles..36

Coming Home..37
Unnamed Creek Behind Cavazos' House...........................38

Fort Spokane..39
A Missouri Drought Morning..41

Hold Onto Fear..42
Storm Front..43

The Loon...44
Current Map for Hugo..45

More and Less... 47
A Drink to the Technician..48

Beside Myself...49
My Favorite Birthday Cakes..50

What I Would Like..52
Know Myself..53

Looking Too Closely at an Apple..54
Du Fu Advice...55

All That Is...56
67..57

Weaving..58
Pounding Language...59

On Water..61
Creek Pen...62

Rising	63
Williams' Chickens	64
Five Flavors of Crazy	65
Dear Reader	66
My Two Sons	67
From My Daughter	69
My Poetry Writing Process by Jim Thielman	71
My Poetry Writing Process by Jim Hanlen	81
Biographical	89

Jim Thielman

When you picture

the rabbit the magician
pulled out of a hat
do you ever wonder
what kind of world it would be
if rabbits pulled magicians
out of tomato patches
or the woman having been
sawed into two pieces
became two women
who didn't take kindly
to being part of an act
and wanted more out of life
and began arguing and
pummeling the magician
with the hat and saw
and maybe even the rabbit,
letting him know
they deserved better
and the audience would
rise up and shout,
throwing fists in the air
because they might not
understand magic
but they did understand
being pummeled and
things not working out
and parties getting ruined
and they weren't paying
good money for that.

Jim Hanlen

Outside Seaside High School

When he misbehaved he was told
"Go outside class and face the ocean."
Minutes later he would forget
why he was sent out there,
not that anyone ever asked.
In a half hour he became two people.
He was the one who talked ocean
looked with blue eyes instead of black
and listened like the wind does.
When he was called back to class
he was the other one.

Jim Thielman

Uncle Fritz

It's one way of praying,
thinking of you years later
and trying to save some gesture.

What did I know?
You lived with us one year
and cut my hair, slanting it across my brow,
a gentle man who drank away a wife and daughters.

The folks helped you sober up,
find a job, and one payday
you brought home presents for each kid.

I see you heading out that evening, shined.
Dad is smiling, proud.
You reach out to shake his hand
and somehow drop a bottle . . .

the shattered glass pokes the eye
of a world he can't control.
He shouts. You leave.
He's sorry how we let you slip away.

In the movie, we would save you just in time,
but two boys, fishing, find you face down in a stream,
your head, a sunken universe for fish to wonder at.

Jim Hanlen

Five Hand Shadows of Birds Thrown Upon the Wall

Uncle would make five of these birds,
one small bird, when he moved
his fist close to the wall,

a big bird, two palms open;
the pigeon beak pecking
was pretty good; my brother

liked wild turkey, a living thing
an eye of light, matching
the bobbing head and our laughter.

The boy who finger traces
a telephone wire under the birds,
that's me. I learned why thin air

meant autumn. Uncle makes an eagle
which seems to come out of nowhere,
wings so large they wrap the room

only a fire engine bell clanging
outside my uncle's house
can break the spell.

Jim Thielman

Dances with Grandma

At ninety-seven she still hears
Jimmy Dorsey and his Band
floating through summer air
at the Northpointe retirement home,

even if the only instrument in sight
is a piano and sometimes the old guy
with his slide trombone.
She glides like a puff of smoke

held here only by my hands
keeping her from flying away
to My Blue Heaven. At five-two,
eyes blue, she tells everyone

over and over that this is her son
and she wonders how his six foot frame
danced out of her tiny self
like some stardust melody of long ago.

Jim Hanlen

River Dance

I ask them to make
the moves of a river.
Some look like they're swimming.
They make long, tall strokes.
I say no, not swimming,
make like the river.
The quiet boy who has his head down
continues to look down
and stand still.
"Stanley what's going on?"
"I'm the moon," he says.
The sunlight is blasting into the room.
"I'm looking down.
I can see the moon
in the fast moving water."

Jim Thielman

Prometheus Resigned

On the bright side no mussel shells
no barnacles scraping my back.
We grow used to pain
as well as freedom.
Chained here I am free.
No need to guess which goddess
I should love
or how to stomach fools.

The theft of fire was a lark
and proved me craftier than Zeus,
whose sense of humor
smacks of vengeance.
If he knew how I like this rock,
perhaps he'd set me free
to fret and stew again.

At night I'm restless,
can't wait for dawn,
for my mind to fly from pain
to far off dreams. I play in a pool
where nymphs glide by
and sing weird songs
that heal with touch of sound.
For them, I would snatch
fire once more and chain
myself to rock, to dreams.

Jim Hanlen

Outside the Gates

> "Outside his poems
> Cavafy does not exist."
> —George Sefiris

You say you want Ithaca.
It's why you're on the road.
Have a beer. Ithaca can wait.

Constantine Tavern stood
at a slight angle to the universe,
An ahistorical tilt.

Write a poem about a Greek door,
a widow looking between a wall,
or an ancient Athenian garden.

Homer was on the right side
of politics. He brought the soldiers
home to Penelope, Telemachus and Argus.

Who learns from history? Look
who is outside the gates now.
Ithaca is not the same.

Jim Thielman

Animals are Buddhists Too

The great egrets
in the delta's shallows
stand and watch
over ripples.
I pedal towards home.
They are home every moment.

Near the main channel
a pelican glides because
it glides. A hatch of insects
draws a flash of trout
into the gleam of sunlight.

Today world peace
didn't happen the way
we might hope
but the spaniel
walking the woman
in white leather
waits while a butterfly
rises off milkweed.

Webs shine in fall grass.
Clouds shed white
strands in blue air as
a praying mantis kneels,
an empty bowl
waiting for breakfast.

Jim Hanlen

Creek Carried the Moon

Deer took a run at it
but the moon's hide
was scratched and scarred,
what an erratic route
he would take down the mountain.

The rabbit took his turn
but he was too slow.
He took all month.
What a disappointment.

The owls distracted it,
chipping away, little bits dropping,
all that was left,
a small jigsaw piece.

So creek carried the moon.
The moon came down the mountain
on creek's back and on time.
Every night creek carried
the moon down to the world.

Jim Thielman

Balm for Blind Hearts

This morning for exercise I pretend to cast
a net across a river and drag it home
until the creaking snakes out of my body,
but no pain floats up my nerves.

No, nothing like what that blind priest suffered.
One thumb slid along the altar and he seeped behind,
carried by osmosis to where we stood
and washed his ancient hands in innocence.
At the consecration, he would raise the cup
on aching joints and grimace when an elbow popped.

What I knew then of sorrow was a blister on my heel,
the rake of blackberry thorns across bare flesh.
I knew blood was redder than wine poured
for blessing. I knew flames burned in hell
and a martyr could cheat the devil and rise to heaven
like smoke from fire-mowed weeds in vacant lots.

What I didn't know was how temptation could
glide across a room in silk, red as a chasuble,
how yellow hair could fade the star of Bethlehem.
I didn't dream how wealth could be so lacquered
its sheen would fool a saint, how guilt
could pepper truth, how lust begets new
saviors on the earth, or how love resurrects
even the shy, even the wise, even the sad
and condescending of this world.

Jim Hanlen

The Blind Priest

No one can hold him between day and night
but God. The meteor showers of Perseids
could have whispered in the blind man's
mind if the light had not given out.
His ears were big, maybe compensation
for no sight. I could have been a priest,
another hand of God. I have short term
memory problems and would have no
trouble dispensing indulgences and penance.
Mortal sins, venial sins, in one ear
and out the other. I would have eaten
the wretchedness before God heard it.

I could have been a priest. I can't sing.
The first time I heard Stabat Mater
the blind priest's dog would moan
in the sacristy like he had heard
it all before at home. The music
of what's heard, the music of what's
not seen. The old dog that does see
but can't bathe, hands off Father
to me every Sunday for Mass.

And the wine. The warm wine.
Father wants me to pour the cruet
of Mogen David over his fingers.
"Hold the water," his hands tell me.

I could have been a priest. I practiced
with my brother pouring water over
my hands. The first time I cleaned

the cruets, that cloying taste, that
syrupy flavor was something I never
found a taste for.

Jim Thielman

Bike Ride on Padero Lane

Wheels pause at a narrow bridge.
A stream finds its way for free
through a private ocean beach where

a sailboat rests, pushed high and dry
by a storm. It happens. We break
loose our moorings and drift

like lost souls. No safe harbor.
A gate through a high wall stands open,
while a bucket loader chunks the craft

into pieces easy to haul away.
Even owners of ocean views will leave
their millions behind. You can weep

a long time over things lost
until you sense a weight lifted.
Now would be the time to let pedals spin

toward nearby orchid farms to see
yellow salted with burgundy,
glory of hibiscus pink played on white.

Jim Hanlen

Professor Gilmore's Breakfast Lecture

"There are no rules except the ones
I make. Butter, hotcakes, syrup,
that's what people will see." He wrapped
his arms around his white cup, a plate of eggs
and toast, and half empty OJ. "These are mine.

What I'm saying, Hold your brush
close. Hold your paints, your canvas
close. Don't let anyone separate you."

He ate his eggs and toast slowly.
He savored the coffee.

Jim Thielman

Do-It-Yourself Traction

It's early morning in 1960, and Dad collapses,
unconscious on the bathroom floor.
Mom calls me to help. I'm 15. Dad wears only a tee shirt.
It's an awkward moment. Back pain knocked him flat.

He comes to. I help him stand, his pelvis so tilted,
if he were an ocean liner, the deck would dump
passengers into the sea. He's like a sailboat with
damaged mast, pulled by forces greater than him,
gusts straining the rigging, or, in his case,
tendon, muscle and bone. We get him to bed,
but soon, he dresses, eats, hobbles to the car
and drives to his auto-body repair shop.

He sees a doctor, who suggests hospital rest and traction.
Dad, who has straightened fenders and frames,
has sailed a boat and winched it on a trailer,
has jacked and pried a dock off a beach
and into water, quizzes the doc about traction,
how it works, how much weight, which way
the tension pulls, then declines the hospital stay,
so he can keep working to feed his wife and kids.

In the basement workshop, he searches and finds
a partly empty paint can. It feels about right.
He gathers some rope, puts on one old boot,
ties it to the handle of the gallon can, and drops it
over the footboard, like a bucket down a well,
but it doesn't work. The weight drags him out of bed.

So he cinches a belt at his waist, ties a rope
from belt to headboard and voila, a steady pull
that lets him sleep through the night. Now it seems,
stars are aligned for a cure, aspirin by day
alcohol with dinner, a weekly Swedish massage,
and the magic paint can, for weeks, tugged
by gravity toward the liquid center of the Earth.

Jim Hanlen

Romanian Circus

Someone has failed to buff the white
high heels of the ringmaster. She
releases the white Pomeranian dogs
leapfrogging over each other,
tracing a line around the ring.
She signals and a dancing pink
poodle enters on its hind legs
and the little dogs take turns
leaping over her. Maybe I'm
too good for this.

This is not my idea of a circus.
My children don't know
there should be stamping elephants,
powerful horses, even a dyspeptic
lion would do. My children are
enthralled. When did I lose my sense
of smell? My children love the smell
of hay bales in ring one, six Pomeranians
sitting on the edge of ring two.

Now the pink beehive ringmaster
moves to the third ring. She parades
around with a live, black metallic rooster
on her left outstretched arm.
My uncle said the bird was
Transylvania Naked Neck
but I said it was spray painted,
light reflecting off his head and chest,
Even hock and shank, spur and claw

gleamed. Why didn't I think
this act didn't fit inside this tent?

She lifted him up to a ten foot high,
gold painted laundry line stretched
out toward the sitting audience.
Little oohs and aahs escaped as he
balanced and walked over to us.

Jim Thielman

This Letter

Let seeds unfold
into reeds that
pounded to papyrus
hold India ink.

Or let photons
shine from screens
and artists shape
fonts like Cambria, Times,
and Verdana
so messages can scatter
across a page.

It's a long journey
from stone and papyrus
to clouds of information
that rain down on us

and maybe find us
finished with dishes
and daily news—

a scatter of words
to brush against
the skin of memory.

Jim Hanlen

Another Way to Read a Poem

Turning clockwise, dancing
From the first word to the last word
On the line. Are you confident
Moving about the poem like a square
Dancer? Next you do-se-do down
To the bottom word on the left
Then grab hands with the word
At the end of the poem. Notice
These words all happy, words
Facing each other. For a moment
The words in the middle seem like
An empty dance floor, where whirling
Dancers have spun apart, have left
Their heart, a picture you can't see
Without giving over your own heart.

Jim Thielman

River Talk

The surface glazes sky
as it shuffles west,
current drawn to the sea.

Cloud on the water
may you cross the Snake River,
slip between mountains,

wander across the Atlantic,
kiss spires in Kiev,
while I in my slow way

dream of sun in Italy,
gold of harvest dusting vineyards,
the moon pulling August

out of the fields, out of the heart
out of a billion eyes
before winter wind calls.

Jim Hanlen

River Breath

The Russian hygienist said, "Your poems
smell strong." "Gum Disease?"
I asked. "You have words

where there should be teeth.
It's just a suggestion. If we
take them out, you will need

a stone dictionary. A just
wildness. Your poems
will lose the river breath."

Jim Thielman

Turtle Man

Some can't survive without music.
The bike rider on State Street
lets beat-up bongo drums
hang off his handlebars

as he heads toward the beach,
where the guitar player
with the grocery cart
spends his afternoons.

Maybe they will get together
and jam a little, the turtle
with his brown dreadlocks,
bound by faded dew rag,

the guitarist a graying blond
with beach-bum wrinkled tan.
The bike is a stuffmobile,
bags hanging everywhere

and all the comforts of home:
bike frame a closet rack,
seat his easy chair, no phone,
only drums to talk out loud.

Jim Hanlen

Looking Under Yeats' Bed

I'm not hurricane material. I'm more
of a dust-up, spin a couple words
and raise a cloud. Younger I would charge
out to the Rattlesnake Mountains.
You wouldn't notice but I took
the tumbleweeds with me. Headlines
like Alaska Oil and Bad Back Cures
were more than rolled directions
and faded newspapers. Ambition?

I'm hollowed out, happy now
to be confused for dust bunnies
under William Yeats' bed. A neighbor
said she thought she recognized me
when she returned from Ireland.

Jim Thielman

EZ Loader 1969

I dip fenders by hand in
a bath of white paint,
thinned until it rolls off steel
like water, but leaves
a sparkling coat
that glows in factory lights.

As fumes intoxicate,
trailer parts rise
from a tank of blue
in a jazzy dance of booms,
tongues and chassis. I dip again,
while the assembly crew's
air guns rattle *con brio*
as they snug lock nuts tight,

while behind me in a blue haze,
arc welders buzz in my ears,
punch presses pound
basso profundo rhythms,
workers feed parts and
toss them into barrels,

until weary with noise
and muddled by fumes.
we go home late Friday
to forget, fall asleep, and
wake each Monday to shine
as bright as clean overalls.

Jim Hanlen

Outside EZ Loader 1966

Night shift is over. God must be muscled,
like us, all those nuts on flanges. Sure there's a few
that fall, obviously not factory warranty. Who said
he doesn't make junk? We choke on our own welding
ether. God's factory without steeples was sure popping
his first week, Most everything does seem screwed true
and tight. God, the best bolt fastener, we add
to his 5-sided, star-flecked bucket of nuts. No wonder
he took a day off, twisted on 4-sided, 5-sided, chrome-light,
chrome-like stars. This guy made the midnight shift glow.
Hard not to brag, write his book, what a guy.

Jim Thielman

Peaceful Valley 1967

Summer days we painted
vintage Spokane houses
and earned money for college.
At dusk in the valley, shaded
by a toll bridge high above,
we cleaned brushes and watered
grass with paint thinner
that peeled away
the postage stamp lawn
of the rental we called home.

Two ways out were uphill
across that bridge to class
or twelve steps to the river,
where once my buddy
sat and watched waves
dance like dead souls
diving into moonlight.

We longed to grow up,
leave our school's cocoon,
though not so suddenly
as the classmate who
during officer training
slipped under those rapids
cold enough to free the spirit.
His body would rise again
by Nine-Mile Falls.

Our lawn stayed brown as jungle
sprayed with agent orange.

Others took a last way out—
red dirt on boots and camouflage
sent home to mix with tears of the wife.
I could have gone
but took student deferments
each time the Draft Board asked.

Now when I see, *Made
in Vietnam*, I wonder if
the seamstress sometimes
tunnels back through memories
to grandparents lost in that war
and if some boy whose battles
could have been mine
made it back.

Jim Hanlen

Water Ave, Peaceful Valley

Dead-end road in the daytime,
sure the river goes on,
but who cares, your front door
opens on empty, the road
a rehearsal for future.
Who would drop kids off here?

        Riverside tarmac
follows the river down
to Bishop's garden. A year
of kneeling will take out
the stones. The poor know
soil and found their place
long ago. Moonlight clears
a mile more

        of peace
in the valley. The wood stove
is a cast iron collie you rub up
against when the cold comes in.
When the war in heaven
came down, the water turned
into stone and saliva, the roll
and spit generating everlasting cold.

    Gone is any sign of Grace
who's back in town.

Jim Thielman

Bliss

It's a name in gold leaf
on a wooden boat.
I've owned boats
and bliss when found
didn't depend on
roaring motors
wrecking quiet
but on openness
to moment by moment
flow of breath,
breeze, leaves, light
and a feeling
I'm riding
here and now
on a boat like Bliss
that floats through
water, solid ground,
clouds and space
so connected
to all I disappear.

Jim Hanlen

Fukushima, Japan 2011

Given this hand I would have folded.
Grateful to have my patch of words
I can name a whole new set
Of 10,000 things, straw, atom, REMS.

The rear card is wild,
The other cards, two months out,
Beta, berries and boron,
Cement and asphalt always in season.

Wave, seismic, containment,
I think I've covered the spread.
How long can anyone hold
That slippery bar of sunlight?

Jim Thielman

Inside Game

When you look closely
at the grain of pine boards
you see dark knots and
around them blond wrinkles
from the weight of branches.
Something small as a seed
became a towering life
bent by storms but
reaching for sun.

In your own life,
moments turned
this way or that because of
weather, friends, accidents,
and yet something unwavering
held sway, something
hidden so deep you
forgot it was there, steady,
lighting the way.

Jim Hanlen

Longevity
> " ... dodging the universal verdict"
> W. Szymborska

Zeno is getting very near the end of his life,
it soon should be within a whisker
after the last two thousand years. So what
is the key to your longevity? Greek rain
and gravel has not diminished your life
or worn out your words.

The wear and tear of family dying,
so many lovers lost, so many fortunes gone,
the world takes its toll. So what
is it that keeps the grinder from milling
your life? I agree Greek olive oil
and retsina are a lubricant of age.

Your photo in the textbook has gone
green eyes to gray. Omega is a backyard
to the neighbor of alpha. The illustration
is an illusion. Metaphysics is half measure.
You see your life is a lifeboat
floating in mercy, bobbing in and out.

Jim Thielman

The Story of My Life

Like confetti it is tumbling,
scraps scattered in a whirlwind
I can't control. A crowd of seagulls
chases juicy bits that drift in air
like parachutes from dandelion puffs.
"This is my life!" I yell, but no one hears.
I gather what I can in my arms.
On one scrap I talk to wife and sons
and on the next I'm rocking on a horse.
Here I am jumping through hoops
and over here I'm dying in a scene
I haven't lived but can't forget.
It's all a jumble. Half the things
I don't recall, facts always twisted
in memory's funhouse mirror.
Shreds slip forever through the air.
I dig for some moment where I
helped a stranger or said a kind word,
but no such luck. The wind is gusting now
and pieces ride a dust devil tower.
I let it go, happy beyond reason,
watching my breaths, those Magellans
of the moment, lifted on their only wings.

Jim Hanlen

Want of Miracles

If angels stood on one foot
could we double the number
that stand on a pin?

This is how it starts, elementary,
and then we visit the graveyard,
the only angel, dumb and cold.

Now I'm older. I'm smarter.
I know about the wild angels,
the ones that get into dancers,

the ones that get into a good poem
if you allow some mystery
and believe in miracles.

The angel that stirs the water
holds the cure, we are told
and we rush in late, lame

much older, no smarter
too slow for inspiration,
oh, for just one more poem.

Jim Thielman

Coming Home

In San Francisco Bay
the breeze ruffles the water
as a ferry boat takes us
from Market Street to Sausalito.

We grab a bite to eat outdoors,
where the restaurant's deck
sits above an older powerboat
tied to a dock. The owner

is eating chowder at the next
table and envying a much larger
sailing yacht, gleaming like
a cover shot as it leans away

from Angel Island to cross
in front of chateau
covered hills of Belvedere.
Next day, we arrive at Pasco's

tiny airport where a small town
wind is blowing. We rescue the car
from long-term parking with dust
so thick, the craters of dried

raindrops look right for planting.
The gloss of big-city life
dulls in the slow quiet of
a Horse Heaven Hills twilight.

Jim Hanlen

Unnamed Creek Behind Cavazos' House

Like a backyard dog, he had a backyard creek,
not a show creek that flashes in sunlight. Tail
wagging, this creek can only burrow down
all day covered up by its own digging,
no big prize, muddy black, a bone hidden creek,

Someone might think it's runoff,
really it's a runaway that has found your house.
All day coming and going and never leaving,
no deep ambition to be a river of rivers,
just a backyard shady creek living in the world's

shadow. This is your fate, my fate, we bend
ourselves to fit in your nightmares and my pain.
What about air and light? Easier to name
the air and light than an unnamed creek,
an unnamed dog that never leaves.

Jim Thielman

Fort Spokane

This wasn't supposed to happen,
Grandson Riley, thirsty and tired,
and me with no money for water
or buckskin trinkets at the visitor center.

We were just going for a stroll
to the end of the sidewalk
at the beachfront park.
The sign in the weeds beckoned.

We climbed switchbacks
to the plateau where Hudson Bay
trappers once set up shop
followed by U.S. soldiers.

I urge Riley to turn back,
but he's been here before and
must see the farthest building,
a stable empty of mules and horses

with its wagon full of firewood
and outside, large corrals.
We cross bunchgrass and wildflowers
taking the shortest route.

No need for fire this summer day.
The sun is slanting into our eyes
and I put my hat on Riley
and carry him half the way back,

from 1850 to the present where
people in Lycra swimsuits laugh.

Water tastes good when you are thirsty,
I say, and Riley answers, *Yes, yes, yes.*

Jim Hanlen

A Missouri Drought Morning

Three dusty turkeys stand on the dusty side
of my sister-in-law's pond. They stand
in white shadows of stone-dry dirt
searching for bugs. A bird she doesn't name
slaps its wings and turns around, swirling dust.
This morning six indigo Buntings,
the ones blackish, Missouri-blue
fly in together, low, parched, looking,
looking for anything not dried up.

From the rim of kitchen light, her pond,
what should be a pond, is down 8 feet,
not so good, you say; not so bad,
she cheers. The bugs have cleared out,
for her, a wood-dry hope. Now she can
clear out the stones and swim next year
without cut feet.

Jim Thielman

Hold Onto Fear

The Russians are already here.
They are the ones flying us into space
and occasionally conquering Crimea.

Who should we fear next?
Perhaps we can fear the Chinese.
They breathe soot and keep running.

And India, the people who
answer all our questions about software.
What will we do if they move to Montana?

Beware of Africans. The Sahara will be
the Saudi Arabia of a solar powered world.

Mexico may soon steal all our workers.
Warming, Canada will replace a sinking Miami.

Syria and Iraq and Iran are full of dangers
and who knows what Madagascar is planning?

Keep running or someone will catch us.
Without our fears, how will we awaken?
With them, how will we fall asleep?

Jim Hanlen

Storm Front

The clouds are like soldiers.
The war just over the next mountain.

The clouds are like soldiers.
Very close on the horizon.

The clouds are like soldiers.
The women speak only of sorrow.

The clouds are like soldiers.
More will be coming.

Jim Thielman

The Loon

I see a wounded loon
        limp across a field.
                No magpie hovers near.

The loon has lost its voice.
        The gray sky offers no escape
                and I no potion to remove

a shotgun pellet from its spine.
        In shrill quiet, I kneel.
                My shoelace came undone.

A cold raindrop drums my neck.
        my backbone, strong and fragile,
                will make it through the day.

A cloud blocks the sun. I shiver and
        my feet want to run.
                Death is life's corona,

it hovers like a dragonfly
        until threads, soft as corn silk,
                break.

Jim Hanlen

Current Map For Hugo

Dick you can't get here
with apologies. I have rum
ricotta and beer to chase
your imagination. You would
have said "Yes, way,"
if I'd said imagination
is faster than light.

Remember Seaside. You sat
in my Nissan, out of breath,
minus a lung, whispering
to the passenger seat
sagging from exhaustion.

I dropped you and your sandals
off at a side street and now
it's time to visit here.

Time and space are never
late or too far,
the science professor says. Time
and space are two seasons
on the Mobius weft
of our gravelly earnest world.
You can ski into spring
or fly into Italy any time
like you've written. Time
is a peek between the pickets.

Emily knew this. Have you seen
her in the blue warp

of eternity? Has she edited
a new atlas of poems?

Stop by. The walkway
is clear. I await your report.
I'll leave the light on.

Jim Thielman

More and Less

more growing in the light
less stumbling in the dark
more joy, less fear

more loving dreams
less failure to connect
more moving, less talking

more seeing into depths
less blinded by the sun
more leaps, less injuries

more meditating on space
less imagining you can't
more listening, less planning

more letting your eyes trace branches
and leaves, less depression
more dancing, less lumbering

more needles per haystack
less failure to see hay is golden
more awake, less caffeinated

more discovery of what's inside
less certainty about anything
more courage, less fear

less left wing right wing
more wings taking flight
more starting, less ending

Jim Hanlen

A Drink To The Technician

End of the block, really ending
in an alley, I found Pound
in Rapallo, a neighborhood bar.
He pretended to take my order
then told the bartender
"a Fascist White Fountain."

Do you know George Lincoln Rockwell?
Study the Pisan Cantos
and drink up. Do you know,
    a swollen magpie in a fitful sun
    half black half white
that's what they served you?

In the dim bar light his lined face,
looked like old leaves pasted ---
(in two years they'd fall away).
The center never holds,
perfect words won't build paradise,
trenches better made than dreams.

Jim Thielman

Beside Myself
    for Colton

A grandfather now,
and sunlight felt
like music dancing.
Maybe, I crossed a border
to a land where thoughts
are water flowing
without words.

Holding grandson,
my clavicle began to ache,
less from the weight,
than a longing to begin again.
The mother's round belly
had unrolled, leaving head
and toe spun into a question:
what will he become?

I ate popcorn and thought
about lives I might have lived.
As his jaundiced skin faded
in special lights, I wanted to say
something for the ages.

It was enough to wave
and nudge a smile
into the curve of lips
that would one day say
whatever would be needed.

Jim Hanlen

My Favorite Birthday Cakes

When I was 25 I worked
at the Spokane Flour Mill.
Once a month they blended
angel food flour for bakeries
and I had to sweep and mop
twice, the flour so fine it
would rise in a cloud when
I walked in to work. The test
kitchen left me a cake.

When I was 15 my friends
chased me from my party
They wanted to spank me,
but I got a piece later.

One day I ate my girlfriend's
birthday cake, special order,
pudding filling, fancy icing
and carrot top design, ate
the whole thing. I had to,
when she didn't come by
to say it was over.

When I was 21 I missed
my cake. I was in Seattle
driving Yellow Cab.

My favorite cake was lemon.
I was 32 and though I enjoyed
others: white and pudding,

chocolate and velvet;
coconut, dark and lime icings.

My wife made this earthquake
cake. Apparently dripping
icing on hot cake breaks
it open, glaze sliding inside.
Sweet, sweet, sweet. A 1964
Commemoration of the earth
shift on 3rd Ave in Anchorage.

When I was 44 I got two
cakes. The bakery said they
made a mistake and I could
have the mistake, no charge.

67. My son makes custom
cupcakes. He whittles
a white queen, bishop
and pawn from cake
with a razor, then burnishing
the crown, mitre and beanie
with dark chocolate.

Jim Thielman

What I Would Like

Patience of weeds, waiting in fog,
never shuttled indoors
to artificial glow and warmth.

Courage of people, homeless,
shrugging off November chill.
Cleansing rain that

falls free from sky
to feathers and farm workers.
Persistence of sunlight, prodding

fog to let go. To be in flow,
body-mind steady from now to now,
and slow move to slow move.

Jim Hanlen

Know Myself

Like creased photos I keep in a box
these gummed-up works are my poems,
the wide-angled ones not so clear.
The good ones, I see people on their knees
rereading like National Geographic maps.

You say you keep your dog
in the backyard. Check out
what's trying to get out of this poem.
My poems are not well-manicured,
so I really like seeing you holding this.

Jim Thielman

Looking Too Closely at an Apple

The freckles on this apple
remind me of the dance of constellations,
the skin's marks irregular, yet patterned
as if Scorpio, Hercules or Cassiopeia
traced their designs on red skin,

along with less famous groupings:
This line of dots I will name Fragment,
and this circle Garland, and this collection
with two stars to mark a wrist and five
to mark fingers will be called Left Hand.

Think of millions of apples with freckles
to map before I tackle pocked skins
of oranges, not to mention florets of broccoli
or the lumpy surfaces of avocados.

When I eat my apple, its stars
will be shining inside me
giving me its all without either of us
being formally introduced.

Will I ever understand my place
in a universe simultaneously designed
and tossed together like a salad?

Jim Hanlen

Du Fu Advice

At this distance it's only words
that let me talk to you. *How do I
describe Tai Mountain?* On one side
there is *concentrated divine*,
where clouds are conceived and born,
on the other a *chest pounding,*
the birds exploding from trees.

All our ambition is in our eyes.
No one climbs either side
and the down wind fills us with regret.
Tell me has Li Bai come this way?

Jim Thielman

All That Is

*We dance round in a ring and suppose
but the Secret sits in the middle and knows.*
          —*Robert Frost*

If we could climb forever
from small to large,
we would rise to stars
with their planet children
and galaxies like countries
and who knows how many
universes, where we
pictured only one.

Meanwhile, we watch while
science dissolves Democritus'
supposedly unchanging atoms
into parts so small they are
waves or quantum bits
and beyond that strings,
thoughts, spirit, dreams.

We are part of some wholeness
so large and far, we can
hardly be blamed for calling,
*mystery, come closer,
whisper my name.*

Jim Hanlen

67

I like
my slouch hat
where rain
can't decide
which side
to run down.

Jim Thielman

Weaving

One thread is nothing,
but enough to hold
the stem of a fuchsia
so its flowers don't
brush passersby
and invite a pruning.

Enough to hold a button,
patch a seam. Of course,
threads, warp and weft,
make the fabric that
covers frames so artists
layer worlds of color

and weave emotions
in waves so fine
they barely hold
the tapestries that trail us
as we walk, flowing
with our deepest desires.

Jim Hanlen

Pounding Language

    for the word hoarder Seamus Heaney

Behind the silhouette of words
"muscle and slur" stand for more
of his salt and slide

available for everything.
If Ireland were a barn,
(not big enough) his seed bag

of words, burlap of lash berries
and red are stacked and the stooping
stiff-legged of the sheep are pasturing.

It's time to call the dogs.
Inside the mudroom are peephole
and coat hook, marks of thick boots,

gray signs of old hats.
Check out the "slime and silver"
of a fatted kitchen, faucet stream

(it all runs clear) over perch.
In the room of "salt and sweat"
he does the best of his ability

(sometimes the light comes off).
My bedroom is no different,
faraway books and babies bouncing,

more words than bad weather.
The water kept in the barn barrow
is the water I pour here

like the clouds rain and roll
and move from left to right.

Jim Thielman

On Water

Old now, we struggle into kayaks
like some birth canal and paddle
out of the lagoon and upriver,
pushing against current in glassy calm.

Upstream, we pause and I
click photos of my wife in a blue vest
and yellow boat and now
a patch of saffron leaves,
casting October glow on water's mirror.

I float away from low afternoon sun,
east, though I have left behind
demands of a direction. The entire bank
lays down its reflection like
one side of its face, or book-matched wood
on some door or table. Here the views
come from two worlds, one where
we could stand, the other where we sink
and join the fishes and olive green
algae on river rocks, tumbled by floods,
and a seasoning of white shells
cast off by freshwater clams.

Heading back, another V winks on water,
a flock of white wings flashing
like marquee lights or diamonds,
as if the sky put on a necklace to meet us.

Jim Hanlen

Creek Pen

My other pen has so much drag,
it seems reluctant to let out
the ink, to push life
into words that speak.

I like this one, my creek pen,
it's clean, thin lines,
my crooked g and slippery s
coming by themselves here.

Jim Thielman

Rising

A change in weather:
cold creeps over skin,
the furnace burns brightly
for awhile and we
take small pleasure
in the warming.

I'm no expert on joy,
but savor fall colors—
red delicious, pumpkin,
green going yellow
or burnt sienna,
the color of cave paintings,
the ancient ones left
before leaving.

Sometimes, I think
how little I have done,
my legacy: a chair I made,
two children with my wife,
a golf swing or two on target,
the tending of things that break,
and this wish for all of us —

peace brothers, sisters,
fruit of blue water
and a long kiss of the sun.

Jim Hanlen

Williams' Chickens

The red wheelbarrow is
American-made, made in New Jersey.
The chickens that are white
are not Tyson or caged
or yellow ones from Arkansas.
You'd say they run free range
but more backyard and free verse.
What is truly remembered
is that it's early morning
and there's glazing on everything,
the morning, the rain, that wheelbarrow
and Williams' white chickens.
So much depends
and it lasts such a short time.

Jim Thielman

Five Flavors of Crazy

As soon as the pain is gone,
we're going to take our meds,
but first our muscles must scream,
until the knots dissolve.

As soon as the war is over,
we're going to stop the killing.
Of course, they'll still want guns,
so they can free more souls.

As soon as we own everything,
we're going to help the poor,
but we're dizzy from playing games.
Don't bother us right now.

As soon as the ocean boils,
we're going to solve the warming,
but don't expect us to change
until our bare feet sizzle.

As soon as our rivals surrender,
we're going to compromise.
Meanwhile, we've automated
the closing of minds to reason.

Jim Hanlen

Dear Reader

I've decided not to write poetry
any longer. It's hopeless. No fabric
can be compared to creek. No rope
looks like creek, laying loose
on the mountainside. I can find
a texture to describe sand sliding
through my fingers, but creek,
it numbs my heart and spills
into my dreams.

                      Creek tries
to empty the mountains, dragging
at something it will never have.
If only creek would drag out
some words. If only I were smart
enough to simply say: The sky
was blue. The mountain opened
a little. The creek that came
ran happy to our town.

Jim Thielman

My Two Sons

Morning light glows around a grove of lilac
where my boys stop to plan their next move.
I snap a picture where they are forever
seven and five, caught in a moment
where blossoms never fall
and they do not grow old.

Magic only works so many miracles.
I sit here old and see them
whispering secrets in my mind.

I pocket the camera as they take off
after a neighbor's cat
stalking a sparrow.

When I was seven, I had a world
full of lilacs and a brother beside me
and vacant lots, where we would
snap milkweed to watch it ooze,
then wash our fingers in dirt.
I recall buttercups, ants nests,
and spider webs laced with dew.

The sparrow on our porch became
the sparrow the cat chased that day,
the sparrow I see out my window now,
the sparrow Shakespeare watched
while a dull teacher droned on and on.
Heraclitus was half right:
Everything changes *and stays the same.*

Mike's and Scott's children walk through
yards with their dogs chasing balls
and their dreams about to blossom.
I think it went that way, one says.
They head out down a long trail.

Jim Hanlen

From My Daughter

My dad is out back with his kids,
that's what my daughter says.
He's counting his stones

and polishing his poems.
He says he's looking for the right word
probably the same word as last week,

that's what she tells her friend.
Then my daughter whispers,
his gold fish is a service animal.

Dad thinks that the fish jumping
out of the bowl at feeding time
wants to help him.

My Poetry Writing Process

Jim Thielman

My Poetry Writing Process

Jim Thielman

     Poetry is fun like golf is fun. I'm a golfer and when people say 'have fun' as I head out on the course, I want to say and sometimes do, "this is golf, it isn't fun, or it's fun for masochists."
     The game of golf is so difficult, such a challenge to your sense of competence. It is great to be outside getting some exercise and testing your ability against a course, but it is also likely to lead to frustration and fits of anger at missed shots or loss of focus that often causes them, or impossible lies.
     Impossible lies would be a good title for a poem, by the way. It is full enough of opportunities to go different directions. It would make for a great game of poetry, a great round, a great course, to keep up the golf metaphor.
     Poetry isn't always as frustrating as golf. If you miss the mark, you can press delete and start again or change a word or line. But getting things right isn't as easy as in golf,

where par for the course is decided. How do you know the poem is finished or as good as you can craft it?

Poetry begins as an incredible contradiction: Create art with words, craft a creative, right-brained masterpiece with clunky tools that inhabit your left brain. Music and art don't deal with this ridiculous starting point. You set out to write something new and surprising with the same words that appear in the daily newspaper or the dictionary.

This is part of the challenge. I tend to have ideas on the daily news, and thoughts about the latest reports from science about our universe, and feelings about what our politicians should be doing but aren't. But to write a poem, I need to let all my beliefs and interests go and free myself up.

That's why I say Impossible Lies is a good title for a poem. It means one thing on the golf course, but taking it out of the golf course context, what does it mean as metaphor? I don't know, but in a poem I could explore possibilities.

So poetry works best when you don't know where it is going until it's done. One dependable way to write surprising poetry that I have found is to start with a list of words and put a word from your list in each line. This solves several problems for writers. You are no longer staring at a blank page and you have set up rules to the game you are about to play.

I think poets who rhyme their lines benefit from this. I'm sure they start some poems with certain rhymes in mind. If I write rhyming lines on purpose I always am writing something humorous. For poems that don't set out to be silly, I seldom use rhyme, although I am aware of the sound of words and will choose language that sounds best to my ear.

Other techniques might be going for a walk or looking out the window and collecting images to use as a starting point. William Stafford pointed out that, since you can't stop thinking, writing is easy if you just lower the bar and put down whatever occurs to you.

Like a cook in an empty kitchen, you need some ingredients. The word list is one way to get started. For me, it seems to trigger the unconscious so that I end up writing things that surprise me, things I didn't plan to write about.

So, a list of words is helpful and I will give an example of what I mean. I've done these word poems several ways. One is to make a list down the left side of a page and write lines that use the word next to that line. The other way is to put a list of words at the top of the page and select from them as you write the poem, maybe using all of them and maybe not.

I once taught high school and had students write poems using tricks like the word list. In that case, I would take several books of modern poetry and flip through them selecting words at random and making a list for the students.

One benefit was how the student's poems were suddenly full of wonderful language they might not have thought to use on their own. Magazines work and any book can be a starting point. Or you can use what comes to mind, since it is much easier to think of things than to think of nothing at all, a state that requires the discipline of a Zen master.

To come up with the list on the next page, I looked around the room and out the windows and at the pictures on the wall. I was in Santa Barbara at the time, but the poem for me ended up set in Richland, Washington, at a house I once lived in. These words offered themselves. These are ordinary words but anyplace is a place to start.

sunlight In the sunlight the world looks golden
garden I find you in the garden
couples where you have picked a couple
apple apples from a tree we planted long ago
sound the sound of bells echoes through the leaves
window In a window I see your face reflected
music as I listen to the music of bees
tea you offer to make me some tea
water with water gathered in moonlight
wind the wind plays in your hair
sailing and sends a leaf sailing our way
slide we slide indoors to the kitchen
glide the day glides into evening
gild the setting sun gilds the window
grow we grow old together in this room

    I don't think of this as great poetry. But it shows how you can produce something from nothing by setting up a list of words and the expectation that you will use them in lines of poetry. Notice how I start out using the words in expected ways, the sunlight is just sunlight, for example. But I suppose I get bored with that and soon couples refers to a couple apples, music becomes the music of bees, sailing doesn't describe sailboats but a leaf, slide is not a playground slide but a way of moving indoors, glide is something the day does, not the people or the falling leaves. I didn't think about this but just put down what occurred to me.

    I went back and reworked the lines a bit making changes you don't see. For one thing, I realized I had placed the 'you' both in the garden and the house at the same time. That could be an option in magical realism, but I didn't intend to go that direction, so I did a little clean up work.

Also, in rewriting or cleaning up individual lines, the tree became one that 'you and I planted' rather than just any tree. That started bringing the people in the poem together, giving them a life, making them a husband and wife, perhaps, making them somewhat like
me and my wife, I suppose, and yet this poem so far is all fiction.

Apples are very difficult to grow without continually spraying them against insects and disease. My wife and I once lived in a house with apple trees and we removed them rather than tend their endless needs.
But there is some emotional truth to the lines above that I relate to in my own life.

Once you have a draft written, you can play with it some more. For example, what if the opening line about the world sunlit and golden was moved somewhere else in the poem. I might also begin tightening the language, cutting unnecessary words. Why not use that title Impossible Lies and see if it changes the poem?

Impossible Lies

I find you in the garden
where you hold apples
picked from a tree
we planted long ago.
Back then, we would
live forever, the children
would never leave.

For a moment, bells echo
through the leaves. I listen
to the music of bees

as they work the roses.
Our sunlit world glows.

Wind plays in your hair
and sends a leaf
sailing our way. Maybe
this is what it means
to have found our
moment of peace.

You offer to make tea
from water gathered
in moonlight. We slide
indoors while the day
glides gently to a close.
we grow old together
in this room.

     So, now the poem has more truth to it, not factual truth but emotional truth. I am sixty-nine as I write this, so a poem dealing with aging is natural for me. The lines have shortened and things have dropped out, including some of the words that started the process going. That's all right. The title for me, bounces off the line about our young selves thinking we would live forever, but it also could fit the 'water gathered in moonlight' a beautiful phrase but not how we make tea in reality. So, the world of the poem is actually its own world, not the one we inhabit but the one that the characters in the poem will inhabit forever.
     With the title, maybe the ending is an impossible lie. No one really grows old in a single room anymore than it happens anywhere else. Yet there is some emotional resonance to a person thinking or feeling this way. It seems right somehow.

If I keep at this poem a few more days, it may ask me to make more changes. I can't write a poem in one go. I can come up with a poem, but it nags at me until I read it again and find something staring at me like I'm an idiot for putting that in there. It is now obvious just how wrong that line or phrase or direction is. It has to go.

Sometimes I meet with other poets and their comments help me see the poem anew and make changes or keep things I was about to change. I revise because I see the lines fresh. Eventually, there is often some electricity of emotion in the poem that tells me it is done. I have put down words that can move a reader—at least me and maybe others.

I did rework the second and third stanza after several days and another person commenting on this poem. The second stanza now ends with the leaf 'sailing our way.' In the third stanza, the couple move indoors in the opening line of the stanza and everything happens there: the tea, the man watching the woman's face reflected in a window, as she prepares dinner.

A version of the reflection line was in the original lines, but dropped out of the first rewrite. I retrieved it and put it to use. I dropped the lines about finding a moment of peace because they seem to tell rather than show. The poem feels peaceful, the scene is quiet and the day is gliding to a close, not slamming any doors.

While the narrator notices the couple is growing old with all of aging's issues, for this moment they feel secure. For me this search for the poem among a thicket of words is the great game of poetry, every much as challenging as golf. Here is the revised poem.

Impossible Lies

I find you in the garden
where you hold apples
picked from a tree
we planted long ago.
Back then, we would
live forever, the children
would never leave.

For a moment, bells echo
through the leaves. I listen
to the music of bees
as they work the roses.
Our sunlit world glows.
Wind plays in your hair
and sends a leaf
sailing our way.

We slide indoors where
you offer me tea from water
gathered in moonlight.
Sunset gilds the windows.
I watch your face,
reflected as you chop
vegetables for dinner.
The day glides to a close.
We grow old together
in this room.

My Poetry Writing Process

Jim Hanlen

My Poetry Writing Process

Jim Hanlen

     My process of writing is to write daily. I'm not a journalist of my inner conflicts and maker of ambition's action plans. I start writing with something seen, a dream recalled, something overheard, a phrase from another poem, then let my mind roam, free-associating. I don't censor what might occur next. This is similar to what I taught my high school Creative Writing class. Later I look it over for images that startle, interesting sounds, and surprises of thought, and write more. I don't have an intention of what I will write. I don't have an audience or publication in mind.   I don't set out to write a political poem or make a social statement or craft a spiritual/religious poem.

In Williams' Chickens for years I wondered what the word depends means in Williams poem: "So much depends/ upon// a red wheel/ barrow// glazed with rain/water// beside the white/ chickens." Only this year I fiddled with it imagining Williams, the physician, in Patterson, NJ making a house call and for one moment I saw him stepping off someone's porch, catching and saving that glimpse of beauty in the backyard.

For me I should be just as surprised as the reader. Poems should have catching images, demonstrate some music (sound patterns, interesting sentence rhythm) and speak "slant" like the sunlight Emily Dickinson saw one winter afternoon. I don't censor what might occur next. This is similar to what I taught my high school Creative Writing class. Later I look it over for images that startle, interesting sounds, and surprises of thought, and write more.

When writing Bird Census in Iraq (see below), the poem originated a few years ago around Christmas when I was intrigued by the idea of counting birds in a war zone. I looked up kinds of birds native in the area, general bird migration patterns and imagined how this might interact. Then I decided to avoid naming any birds in the poem. Origins and first causes always interest me. First birds, first scripture. One surprising image I liked was "drive-by music." The yearly entries were written at different weeks and I realized later they could be of one piece.

Iraqi Bird Census
2002

Mesopotamia birds are old. Oldest.
Label them Assyrian or Babylonian,
it really makes no difference.
They're all descended from Eden,

where birds were too many to count.

Summer on the Euphrates, winter
at the Tygris. Why would you leave?
Today they're ascending to heaven
the one day we count scripture.

2004

We count the foolish ones. There
are only the smart ones and the foolish.
These are wild times. Smart birds
have left. The foolish are on the fence,
gawking, hanging on and shitting.

The foolish sing at every little thing:
parades, women with dripping buckets,
explosions that look like sunrise
and need some kind of song.

The foolish are happy to take
the left-over bread, the soiled lamb
and the rotted secrets under uniforms.

2005
Sometimes they're counted twice.
When you see them here
they're Shia. Over that wall
over there they'll be Sunni.
But fat chance,
they've turned off the water.
And do you see any trees?
What you're hearing is American
music, the drive-by kind.
The ones, those overhead, headed east,
how many would you say,

they'll be counted again.
Dress them up as Kurds
The Turks will see them as Turks
No Kurdistan, no birds,
Some days, birds are more than birds.

2006

Not many. Not as many

as you'd expect. The male
birds
the ones that sing in old
Persian

have been run off. Those
birds

that seem to fly above it
all

they're not from Iraq.
The sleek

ones are from those high rises
in Abu Dhabi,

the rest from the Emirates

probably wintering in
Turkey

and Greece. If you flew over
Baghdad,

checked out those

courtyards

only a few shade trees
left,

those black birds walking
around

look like lost ladies in
burqas.

Biographical

Jim Hanlen married Brenda in 1969. They have two children and one grandchild. Jim taught high school in Washington state 20 years before retiring. He moved to Anchorage, Alaska where his wife teaches and does her fine art.

Jim received an NEA fellowship for a month residence at Centrum Washington. In 1984 Jim published 17 Toutle River Haiku about the Mt. St. Helens eruption. He has other poems anthologized in *Weathered Poetry, Season of Dead Water, Poisoned Poetry, Retirement and GRRR*. Other poems have been printed in *English Joural, Cirque, TapJoe and Salal Review*

Jim Thielman married Pat in 1967. They have two children and five grandchildren. Jim taught high school in Richland, Washington for seven years. He worked for Hanford companies for over 20 years including 17 years at Battelle Pacific Northwest National Laboratory. He has written a humor book, *The Theory of Wrong* with Bob Heck, published articles about flying in NASA's "Vomit Comet" in area newspapers, won a poetry contest at Gonzaga University, and published poems in *Cirque*. He studied for a year at Iowa's Writer's Workshop. He lives along the Columbia River, in Richland, Washington.

Made in the USA
Charleston, SC
13 August 2015